Seamless Knits
for Posh Pups

Sharon Sebrow

Martingale®
Create with Confidence

Dedication

For my brother, Joel, of blessed memory.
You taught me the importance of green,
fuzzy yarn.

Martingale®
19021 120th Ave. NE, Ste. 102
Bothell, WA 98011-9511 USA
ShopMartingale.com

Printed in China
20 19 18 17 16 15   8 7 6 5 4 3 2 1

Library of Congress Cataloging-in-Publication Data is available upon request.

ISBN: 978-1-60468-515-2

Mission Statement

Dedicated to providing quality products and service to inspire creativity.

Credits

PUBLISHER AND CHIEF VISIONARY OFFICER
Jennifer Erbe Keltner

EDITORIAL DIRECTOR
Karen Costello Soltys

DESIGN DIRECTOR
Paula Schlosser

ACQUISITIONS EDITOR
Karen M. Burns

PRODUCTION MANAGER
Regina Girard

TECHNICAL EDITOR
Amy Polcyn

COVER AND INTERIOR DESIGNER
Connor Chin

COPY EDITOR
Marcy Heffernan

PHOTOGRAPHER
Brent Kane

ILLUSTRATOR
Kathryn Conway

Seamless Knits
for Posh Pups

Contents

Why Seamless?   6

The Right Fit   8

Quick Tips   9

12

Sparkle

15

Otis

19

Chip

22

Rocky

25

Erin

29

Buddy and Diamond Girl

32

Rosco

35

Skye

38

Max

41

Tiffany

44

Cecil

48

Waldo

52

Taffy

55

Buttercup

Basic Stitches   58

Abbreviations   60

Helpful Information   61

Acknowledgments   62

About the Author   64

Why Seamless?

The saying goes, "It is about the journey, not the destination." But let's face it, if there's a shortcut, we'll take it, right?

I love to lose myself in a great knit as much as anyone, but seaming the pieces together is far from my favorite part. Seamless knitting is an opportunity to enjoy the knitting part of the project and bind off with a completed, three-dimensional, wearable garment! Finished, with a capital *F*. And, when knitting top down, there is the added bonus of being able to try your garment on before you bind off to check that the lengths of the sleeves, or the bodice, are just right. Needless to say, once introduced to it, I fell in love with seamless, top-down knitting.

When I needed a sweater for my new puppy, I was disappointed that I was not able to find patterns for dog sweaters that used seamless construction. So, I picked up my calculator, took my new dog's measurements, and worked out some seamless dog-sweater designs. In *Seamless Knits for Posh Pups,* I share with you two basic styles of dog sweaters using seamless construction: a versatile sleeveless sweater and a raglan-sleeve sweater.

The sleeveless style can easily have sleeves added, as I did with "Chip" (page 19). It can also be made either from the top down or from the bottom up. Working from the bottom allows you to take advantage of decorative scallops that develop from the cast-on edge as a result of certain stitch patterns, such as in "Buttercup" (page 55).

The raglan style offers an automatic sleeve, which can easily be worked short, as in "Taffy" (page 52), or long as in "Waldo" (page 48 and shown above), to fit your dog's leg length perfectly.

While the styles are basic, I varied the yarn weights and textures to give each sweater a unique look. Beyond that, I also changed things up by including a wide range of knitting techniques, such as textured fabrics using a combination of knits and purls, slipped stitches, cables, lace, and beading.

You'll also find tips designed to help you knit in the round, follow charts, and knit lace like a pro. Let these simple projects lead you to new techniques and inspire you to go beyond the quick dog sweater, venturing into seamless knitting for the humans in your life. Meanwhile, your favorite posh pup will be dressed in style!

Naming is a difficult task. After all, it took seven of us and three days to name our beloved golden-doodle, Hailey. You look at the pet, play with the pet, see how he or she makes you feel, and then give the pet a name. Thinking it would be clever to use actual dog names for the projects, I paired the feeling of each project to names which evoked that same feeling. I hope you enjoy!

Kudos to the Models

Many thanks to Ally, Brusier, Grayson, Hera, Koki, Maggie, Rufus, Sammee, Scooter, Stelios, and Tiki (and all their owners) for taking time out of their busy schedules to model the sweaters in this book.

The Right Fit

From breed to breed, leg and body lengths can vary and may not be proportional to specific chest circumferences. Therefore, the project patterns in this book use a basic formula taking into consideration the knitted gauge of the project yarn, stitch-pattern repeats, and a common size structure (Small, Medium, Large) for dogs that range in size from under 10 pounds to about 30 pounds. The table below shows the general measurements used to calculate project sizes. Measure your dog to determine which size to knit.

Making Adjustments

Understanding that your dog may be long and skinny like a dachshund, or have a wide, short neck and barrel chest like a pug, I encourage you to make changes to the project patterns to ensure the proper fit.

Length is the simplest thing to adjust, so choose the size structure that fits your dog's neck and chest circumferences best. If your dog is toward the high end of a size or if you want a looser fit, as you may with fluffier dogs, you might want to size up. But realize there is a lot of give and stretch with the sweaters, so a smaller size may still fit around a larger dog.

To personalize the fit for your dog, you can change the number of cast-on stitches for a wider or narrower neck, increase or decrease stitches for a wider or narrower chest width, and add rows to adjust length. However, some projects have a stitch or color pattern that requires a specified number of stitches or rows to complete a repeat. Keep this in mind when making adjustments.

If you need information on particular techniques used in the patterns, see "Basic Stitches" on page 58. I've also included "Quick Tips" on page 9, so you might want to look those over before beginning, even if you're a more experienced knitter.

Approximate Dog Measurements

Size	Weight	Garment Length	Neck Circumference	Chest Width	Neck to Front Leg	Garment Leg Opening	Chest Circumference
Small	Under 10 lbs	11"	9" to 10"	4½"	1¾"	1½"	13" to 14"
Medium	10 to 20 lbs	14"	11" to 12"	5¾"	2¾"	2"	17" to 18"
Large	20 to 30 lbs	17"	13"	7"	3¼"	2½"	19" to 20"

Small *Medium* *Large*

These helpful hints will guide you to create a perfect sweater for your pampered pet. Read them carefully before beginning, particularly if you are new to circular knitting. The projects in this book make extensive use of knitting in the round, both on circular and double-pointed needles. While this technique isn't difficult, there are "tricks of the trade" that can make it easier and produce superior results. Likewise, if you are new to reading charts, short rows, or lifelines, there are useful tidbits here for you as well.

Joining in the Round

To avoid a gap at the first stitch when joining in the round, work with double-pointed needles or circular needles and hold the needles with the working yarn coming off the last cast-on stitch on the right-hand needle. The left-hand needle tip will have the first cast-on stitch (a slipknot when using the knitted cast-on technique). With the tip of the right-hand needle, slip the first cast-on stitch from the left-hand needle onto the right-hand needle. With the tip of the left-hand needle, lift the last cast-on stitch from the right-hand needle over the first cast-on stitch, keeping the first cast-on stitch on the tip of the right-hand needle and the last cast-on stitch on the tip of the left-hand needle. The last cast-on stitch now becomes the first stitch to knit into. Pull the working yarn so it's tight around the stitch it has crossed over. This will help keep a gap from forming.

Taking Care Not to Twist Stitches

The cast-on stitches often have a mind of their own and can twist themselves around the needles in a coil. Place the needles on a flat surface and look at the spine of the cast-on stitches. It should be straight along the inside edge of the needle(s) and not spirally twisted around. Also, look between the double-pointed needles to be sure they aren't rotated. Once the spine is straight, you're ready to join in the round and start knitting.

Switching from Double-Pointed Needles to Circular Needle

When you've increased enough stitches to fit on a circular needle, it's not necessary to transfer them to the double-pointed needles one at a time. Rather, knit directly from the double-pointed needles onto a circular needle of an appropriate size.

Reading Charts

Because the specific construction of projects in this book combines both knitting in the round and knitting back and forth, I have provided charts for all stitch patterns to avoid confusion. Follow the stitch chart from right to left when working the right side and left to right when working the wrong side.

Working Partial Rows

There is no need for stitches to be moved back and forth onto holders. Per the pattern, knit the necessary number of stitches row by row, turning your work after working the number of stitches specified. All unused stitches will simply remain, unworked, on the cable of the circular needle.

Working with Two Circular Needles at the Same Time

With stitches separated on different circular needles, use both ends of the same circular needle. Work the stitches on that circular needle to the end, drop both ends of the circular needle (placing point protectors if needed), pick up the next circular needle with the next group of stitches, and work to the end of that group.

Adding Sleeves

The "Chip" sweater (page 19) features sleeves that are added onto an

otherwise finished sleeveless sweater. The same technique can be used to add sleeves of any length to any of the sleeveless, top-down patterns. The gauge may be different, so keep that in mind when picking up stitches around the leg opening.

Lifelines

Mistakes happen, and when working with increases, decreases, and yarn overs, it's very hard to be sure you've picked up all the stitches correctly after ripping out full rows. This is where a lifeline can really save you.

Insert a lifeline at the beginning of a repeat or section. Thread waste yarn through the live stitches on your needles, but *do not* remove the stitches from the needle. The stitches are knit regularly, with the waste yarn pushed down and out of the way, ignored as if it was not there. If rows need to be ripped, you can rip down to the waste yarn. The lifeline will catch all the stitches at that row. The live stitches can easily be slipped onto needles, and you can begin knitting again as if nothing had ever happened.

Closing Gaps between Double-Pointed Needles

It's common for a gap to form between the last stitch of one double-pointed needle and the first stitch of the next double-pointed needle. To make this less noticeable, work a few extra stitches from the next needle onto the previous needle every three to five rounds, shifting the position between the needles. Any minor gaps will be redistributed and virtually invisible when the garment is completed.

Sparkle

Let your pup show her moves while showing off this lovely basic sleeveless sweater, "Sparkle." If you're new to knitting in the round or top-down construction, this basic pattern is a good place to start. Choose either the turned-down turtleneck or the shorter crewneck version.

Skill level: Easy ●■□◗

Construction: Sleeveless top down

Sizes

Small (Medium, Large)

Finished Measurements

Length: 11 (14, 17)"

Neck circumference: 9 (11½, 13¼)"

Chest width: 4½ (5½, 6¾)"

Chest circumference: 13½ (17¾, 19¾)"

Note: Sizes above are approximate. Slight changes in number of stitches and/or rows have been made to accommodate the stitch pattern and/or gauge. The garment will stretch. For additional sizing information, see "The Right Fit" (page 8).

Materials

1 (2, 2) skein of Martha Stewart Crafts extra soft wool blend from Lion Brand Yarn (65% acrylic, 35% wool; 100 g; 164 yds) in color Lilac (❹)

US size 7 (4.5 mm) double-pointed needles and 16" to 22" circular needle, or size needed to obtain gauge

US size 5 (3.75 mm) double-pointed needles and 16" to 22" circular needle

US size 8 (5 mm) double-pointed needles (for turtleneck option only)

2 stitch markers in different colors

Tapestry needle

Gauge

18 sts and 25 rows = 4" in St st using size 7 needles

Turtleneck *Only*

With size 8 needles, CO 40 (52, 60) sts and distribute onto 3 dpns. Join in the round, taking care not to twist sts, and PM A to note beg of rnd. Work in K2, P2 rib for 8 (10, 12) rnds. Change to size 5 needles, and cont in patt for an additional 7 (9, 11) rnds. Beg "Neck to Leg Opening" section below.

Crewneck *Only*

With smaller needles, CO 40 (52, 60) sts and distribute onto 3 dpns. Join in the round, taking care not to twist sts, and PM A to note beg of rnd. Work in K2, P2 rib for 8 (10, 12) rnds.

Neck to Leg Opening

Change to circular needle when needed.

Next rnd: Change to larger needles, sl marker A, M1L, PM B, knit to end of rnd.

Next rnd: Sl marker A, M1L, knit to marker B, M1R, sl marker B, knit to end of rnd.

Rep last rnd until there are 21 (25, 31) sts between markers.

Work even for 2 (4, 5) rnds—61 (77, 91) sts.

Chest

Separate chest and back sts for leg openings as follows: sl marker A, knit to marker B. Turn work. Leave rem sts unworked for back.

Cont to work chest sts in St st, turning at end of each row, for 10 (12, 16) rows, ending with a RS row. Cut yarn, leaving approx 8" tail.

Back

Join working yarn to back, starting on RS row. Cont to work back sts in St st for 10 (12, 16) rows, ending with a WS row. Turn work.

Join to Work in the Round

Next rnd: Knit across back to marker A. Join back to chest, keeping marker in place, knit to marker B, join chest to back, keeping marker in place, knit to end of rnd.

Knit 8 rnds.

For male dogs only, beg chest rib now. For female dogs, work 8 more rnds in St st, and then beg chest rib.

"Sparkle" in alternate colorway, Dusty Purple

This pattern's simplicity offers a perfect opportunity to work with a wonderful self-striping novelty yarn, like Lion Brand Yarn's Keppi.

Chest Rib

Optional: For a tighter chest rib, work chest sts with smaller circular needles and back sts with larger circular needles. See "Working with Two Circular Needles at the Same Time" (page 10). In this case, markers can be removed when sts are separated on the two circular needles.

Next rnd: Sl marker A, work in P1, K1 rib (beg and end with purl), sl marker B, knit to end of rnd.

Rep for 7 more rnds. Remove marker A. BO 21 (25, 31) chest sts in patt. Remove marker B—40 (52, 60) sts.

Complete the Back

Cont working back and forth in patt until piece measures 9½ (12½, 15½)" from bottom edge of collar rib or until sweater is 1½" shorter than desired length.

Change to smaller needles, work in K2, P2 rib for a total of 9 rows.

BO in patt.

Weave in all ends.

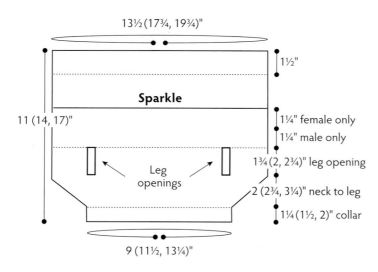

13½ (17¾, 19¾)"

1½"

Sparkle

11 (14, 17)"

1¼" female only

1¼" male only

1¾ (2, 2¾)" leg opening

Leg openings

2 (2¾, 3¼)" neck to leg

1¼ (1½, 2)" collar

9 (11½, 13¼)"

Otis

Any dog can strut with attitude when wearing "Otis," a hoodie sweater with kangaroo pocket. The hood can be worn over the head for added warmth, or lengthened to be worn back over the shoulders.

Skill level: Experienced ●■■●

Construction: Sleeveless top down

Sizes

Small (Medium, Large)

Finished Measurements

Length: 11 (14, 17)"

Neck circumference: 9 (12, 13)"

Chest width: 4¼ (5¾, 6¾)"

Chest circumference: 13¼ (17¾, 19¾)"

Hood: 4½ (6, 8)"

Note: Sizes above are approximate. Slight changes in number of stitches and/or rows have been made to accommodate the stitch pattern and/or gauge. The garment will stretch. For additional sizing information, see "The Right Fit" (page 8).

Materials

Vanna's Choice from Lion Brand Yarn (100% acrylic; 100 g; 170 yds) (4)

MC 1 skein in color Aqua

CC1 1 skein in color Linen

CC2 1 skein in color Fern

US size 9 (5.5 mm) double-pointed needles and 16" to 22" circular needle, or size needed to obtain gauge

US size 7 (4.5 mm) double-pointed needles and 16" to 22" circular needle

2 stitch markers in different colors

4 point protectors

Crochet hook

Waste yarn

Tapestry needle

Gauge

16 sts and 22 rows = 4" in St st using size 9 needles

Hood

With larger dpns use crocheted provisional CO (see "Provisional Cast On," page 58), to CO 16 (22, 23) sts with waste yarn. Place point protector at beg of CO and another point protector on end of second dpn. Use these 2 needles to work next 5 rows.

> **Rows 1, 3, and 5 (RS):** With MC, knit.
>
> **Rows 2 and 4:** Purl.
>
> Remove waste yarn and sl 16 (22, 23) live sts to second, now empty, needle with point protector, including extra loop at end that holds only end of waste yarn—32 (44, 46) sts. Working yarn will be situated between tips of 2 dpns. With a third dpn, knit new sts to

end of row. Turn work. *Note:* Do not remove point protectors. Needles with point protectors denote the ends of the rows.

Next row: Purl sts on first needle, use newly open needle to cont to purl sts from second needle. (Pull first stitch of second needle tightly to avoid loose sts between needles.) Turn at end of row.

Cont working St st back and forth across the 2 dpns until piece measures 4½ (6, 8)" from fold at hood top, ending with a WS row—32 (44, 46) sts.

Optional: Work 1" longer for hood if it will be worn pulled back over the shoulders and tacked in place.

Collar

Changing to smaller dpns and CC1, cont to work back and forth in rows as follows:

Row 1: K1, M1L, *K1, P1; rep from * until 1 st rem, M1R, P1.

Row 2: Work in K1, P1 rib.

Row 3: P1, M1L, *P1, K1; rep from * until 1 st rem, M1R, K1.

Row 4: Work in P1, K1 rib.

Size Large only

Next row: K1, M1L, *K1, P1; rep from * until 1 st rem, M1R, P1.

Next row: Work even in rib patt.

All Sizes

Join in the round and PM A to denote beg of rnd. Work even in patt for 1 (2, 3) rnds—36 (48, 52) sts.

"Otis" in alternate colorway, Scarlet

Stripes

Change to CC2. Change colors in sequence MC, CC1, CC2 every 4 rnds/rows. Change colors at marker A until chest and back are joined; thereafter, change at marker B.

Neck to Leg Opening

Change to circular needle when needed.

Next rnd: Change to larger needles, sl marker A, M1L, PM B, knit to end of rnd.

Next rnd: Sl marker A, M1L, knit to marker B, M1R, sl marker B, knit to end of rnd.

Rep last rnd until there are 17 (23, 27) sts between markers.

Work even for 2 (3, 4) rnds. Note last rnd of color sequence worked—53 (71, 79) sts.

Chest

Separate chest and back sts for leg openings as follows: sl marker A, knit to marker B. Turn work. Leave rem sts unworked for back.

Cont to work chest sts back and forth in St st, for 8 (10, 14) rows, ending with a RS row. Cut yarn, leaving approx 8" tail.

Back

Join working yarn to back, starting on RS row. Cont to work back sts in St st for 8 (10, 14) rows, ending with a WS row. Turn work.

Join to Work in the Round

All color changes will now be made after marker B.

Next rnd: Knit across back to marker A. Join back to chest, keeping marker in place. Knit to marker B. Join chest to back, keeping marker in place, knit to end of rnd.

Knit 0 (2, 4) rnds.

Next rnd: For pocket prep, knit to marker B, K12 (16, 17), P12 (16, 18), K12 (16, 17) to end of rnd.

For male dogs only, beg chest rib now. For female dogs, work 8 more rnds, and then begin chest rib.

Chest Rib

Optional: For tighter chest rib, work chest sts with smaller circular needles and back sts with larger circular needles. See "Working with Two Circular Needles at the Same Time" (page 10). In this case, markers can be removed when sts are separated on the two circular needles.

Next rnd: Sl marker A, work in P1, K1 rib (beg and end with purl), sl marker B, knit to end of rnd.

Rep for 6 more rnds. Remove marker A. BO 17 (23, 27) chest sts in patt. Remove marker B—36 (48, 52) sts.

Complete the Back

Work back and forth in rows in St st until back measures 3" from pocket prep row, ending with a WS row. Place point protectors on both ends of needle.

Pocket

With larger needles and separate ball of yarn, RS facing you, and collar end down, PU and knit 11 (15, 17) sts from purled sts in pocket prep rnd, turn work.

Row 1: K3, purl until 3 sts rem, K3.

Row 2: K3, M1L, knit until 3 sts rem, M1R, K3.

Rep last 2 rows 4 times more—21 (25, 27) sts.

Work even for 5 rows, ending with a WS row.

Join Pocket to Back

Next row: Hold back needle and let pocket dpn hang; K7 (11, 12) from back needle. Hold pocket needle together with and in front of back needle. Work next 21 (25, 27) sts from front and back needles together by inserting RH needle into first st on each needle at same time, K2tog. Rep across rem pocket sts, knit to end of row. Turn work.

Cont working back and forth in patt until piece measures 9½ (12½, 15½)" from bottom edge of collar rib or until sweater is 1½" shorter than desired length.

Change to smaller needles, work in K1, P1 rib for a total of 8 rows.

BO in patt.

Weave in all ends.

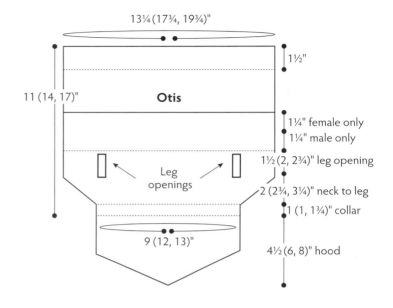

13¼ (17¾, 19¾)"

11 (14, 17)"

Otis

1½"

1¼" female only
1¼" male only

1½ (2, 2¾)" leg opening

Leg openings

2 (2¾, 3¼)" neck to leg

1 (1, 1¾)" collar

9 (12, 13)"

4½ (6, 8)" hood

Chip

Your dog can be the mascot when wearing team colors in "Chip," a letterman sweater. Adding sleeves gives this sweater a totally sporty look!

Skill level: Easy ●■□◖

Construction: Top down with sleeves

Sizes

Small (Medium, Large)

Finished Measurements

Length: 11 (14, 17)"

Neck circumference: 9 (12, 13)"

Chest width: 4¼ (5¾, 6¾)"

Chest circumference: 13¼ (17¾, 19¾)"

Note: Sizes above are approximate. Slight changes in number of stitches and/or rows have been made to accommodate the stitch pattern and/or gauge. The garment will stretch. For additional sizing information, see "The Right Fit" (page 8).

Materials

Vanna's Choice from Lion Brand Yarn, (100% acrylic; 100 g; 170 yds) (■4■)

MC 1 (2, 2) skein in color Colonial Blue

CC 1 (1, 1) skein in color Lamb

US size 9 (5.5 mm) double-pointed needles and 16 to 22" circular needle, or size needed to obtain gauge

US size 7 (4.5 mm) double-pointed needles and 16" to 22" circular needle

2 stitch markers in different colors

Tapestry needle

Gauge

16 sts and 22 rows = 4" in St st using size 9 needles

Collar

With smaller needles and MC, CO 36 (48, 52) sts and distribute onto 3 dpns. Join in the round, taking care not to twist sts, and PM A to denote beg of rnd. Work in K1, P1 rib for 2 rnds.

Change to CC, work in patt for 3 rnds.

Change to MC, work in patt for 2 (3, 2) rnds.

Size Large only: Change to CC, work in patt for 3 rnds.

Neck to Leg Opening

Change to circular needle when needed.

Next rnd: Change to larger needles, sl marker A, M1L, PM B, knit to end of rnd.

Next rnd: Sl marker A, M1L, knit to marker B, M1R, sl marker B, knit to end of rnd.

Rep last rnd until there are 17 (23, 27) sts between markers—53 (71, 79) sts.

Work even for 2 (4, 5) rnds.

Chest

Separate chest and back sts for leg openings as follows: sl marker A, knit to marker B. Turn work. Leave rem sts unworked for back.

Cont to work chest sts in St st, turning at end of each row, for 8 (10, 14) rows, ending with a RS row. Cut yarn, leaving approx 8" tail.

Back

Join working yarn to back, starting on RS row. Cont to work back sts in St st for 8 (10, 14) rows, ending with a WS row. Turn work.

Join to Work in the Round

Knit across back to marker A. Join back to chest, keeping marker in place, knit to marker B, join chest to back, keeping marker in place, knit to end of rnd.

Knit 5 rnds.

For male dogs only, beg chest rib now. For female dogs, work 7 more rnds, and then begin chest rib.

Chest Rib

Optional: For a tighter chest rib, work chest sts with smaller circular needles and back sts with larger circular needles. See "Working with Two Circular Needles at the Same Time" (page 10). In this case, the markers can be removed when the sts are separated on the two circular needles.

Next rnd: Sl marker A, work in P1, K1 rib (beg and end with purl), sl marker B, knit to end of rnd.

Rep for 6 more rnds. Remove marker A. BO 17 (23, 27) chest sts in patt. Remove marker B—36 (48, 52) sts.

Complete the Back

Cont working back and forth in patt until piece measures 9½ (12½, 15½)" from bottom edge of collar rib or until sweater is 1½" shorter than desired length.

Change to smaller needles, work in K1, P1 rib for 2 rnds.

Change to CC, work in patt for 2 rnds.

Change to MC, work in patt for 2 rnds.

Change to CC, work in patt for 2 rnds.

Change to MC, work in patt for 1 rnd.

BO in patt.

Weave in all ends.

Sleeves

With larger needles and CC, RS facing you, start at bottom of leg opening, and PU and knit 19 (23, 27) sts evenly around, PM A on needle before first stitch to note beg of rnd and PM B after 8th (10th, 12th) stitch.

Knit for 6 (8, 10) rnds, keeping markers in place.

Decrease rnd: Knit to 2 sts before marker, ssk, K3, K2tog, knit to end of rnd (2 sts dec).

Knit 2 (3, 4) rnds. Rep dec rnd above.

Large size only

Knit 2 rnds. Rep dec rnd above—15 (19, 21) sts.

Work even for 2 (4, 6) rnds, or to 1" from desired sleeve length.

All sizes

On last rnd, dec 1 st—14 (18, 20) sts.

Cuff Rib

Change to smaller needles and MC, work in K1, P1 rib for 2 rnds.

Change to CC, work in patt for 2 rnds.

Change to MC, work in patt for 1 rnd.

BO in patt.

Weave in all ends.

Rep for second sleeve.

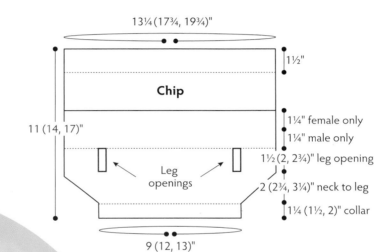

13¼ (17¾, 19¾)"

Chip

1½"

11 (14, 17)"

1¼" female only
1¼" male only
1½ (2, 2¾)" leg opening
2 (2¾, 3¼)" neck to leg
1¼ (1½, 2)" collar

Leg openings

9 (12, 13)"

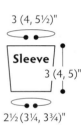

3 (4, 5½)"

Sleeve

3 (4, 5)"

2½ (3¼, 3¾)"

Rocky

Cozy and warm, "Rocky" is a cabled sweater, ready for outside wear. Working cables along both sides of the back give a balanced and classy look for male or female dogs.

Skill level: Easy ●■□◖

Construction: Sleeveless top down

Sizes

Small (Medium, Large)

Finished Measurements

Length: 11 (14, 17)"

Neck circumference: 10 (12, 13¼)"

Chest width: 4½ (5¾, 6¾)"

Chest circumference: 14½ (18, 20)"

Note: Sizes above are approximate. Slight changes in number of stitches and/or rows have been made to accommodate the stitch pattern and/or gauge. Garment will stretch. For additional sizing information, see "The Right Fit" (page 8).

Materials

1 (2, 2) skein of Jiffy from Lion Brand Yarn (100% acrylic; 85 g; 135 yds) in color Country Green (🧶 **5**)

US size 10 (6 mm) double-pointed needles and 16" to 22" circular needle, or size needed to obtain gauge

US size 8 (5 mm) double-pointed needles and 16" to 22" circular needle

4 stitch markers in 3 different colors (markers A and B should be different, C and D can be the same color)

Cable needle

Tapestry needle

Gauge

14½ sts and 18 rows = 4" in St st using size 10 needles

Pattern Stitch

See chart on page 24.

Collar

With smaller needles, CO 36 (44, 48) sts and distribute onto 3 dpns. Join in the round, taking care not to twist sts, and PM A to note beg of rnd. Work in K2, P2 rib for 6 (7, 9) rnds.

Neck to Leg Opening

Change to circular needle when needed.

Change to larger needles, sl marker A, M1L, PM B, K5 (9, 11), PM C, work row 1 of chart, PM D, K5 (9, 11) to end of rnd.

Next rnd: Sl marker A, M1L, knit to marker B, M1R, sl marker B, K5 (9, 11), sl marker C, work next row of chart, sl marker D, K5 (9, 11) to end of rnd.

Rep last rnd until there are 17 (21, 25) sts between markers.

Work even for 1 (1, 1) rnd. Note last row worked of chart—53 (65, 73) sts.

Chest

Separate chest and back sts for leg openings as follows: sl marker A, knit to marker B. Turn work. Leave rem sts unworked for back.

Cont to work chest sts in St st, turning at end of each row, for 6 (8, 12) rows, ending with a RS row. Cut yarn, leaving approx 8" tail.

Back

Join working yarn to back, starting on RS row. Work back sts in patt for 6 (8, 12) rows, ending with a WS row. Turn work.

Join to Work in the Round

Next rnd: Work in patt across back to marker A. Join back to chest, keeping marker in place, knit to marker B, join chest to back, keeping marker in place, work in patt to end of rnd.

Work 4 rnds in patt.

For male dogs only, beg chest rib now. For female dogs, work 6 more rnds, and then begin chest rib.

Chest Rib

Optional: For tighter chest rib, work chest sts with smaller circular needles and back sts with larger circular needles. See "Working with Two Circular Needles at the Same Time" (page 10). In this case, markers can be removed when sts are separated on the two circular needles.

Next rnd: Sl marker A, work in P1, K1 rib (beg and end with purl), sl marker B. Work in patt to end of rnd.

Rep for 5 more rnds. Remove marker A. BO 17 (21, 25) chest sts in patt. Remove marker B—36 (44, 48) sts.

Complete the Back

Cont working back and forth in patt until piece measures 9½ (12½, 15½)" from bottom edge of collar rib or until sweater is 1½" shorter than desired length.

Change to smaller needles, work in K2, P2 rib for a total of 7 rows.

BO in patt.

Weave in all ends.

Rocky

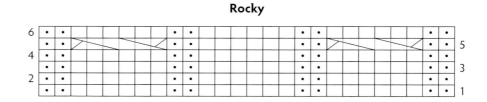

Legend

☐ K on RS, P on WS

• P on RS, K on WS

⬭ Sl 3 to cn and hold in front, K3, K3 from cn

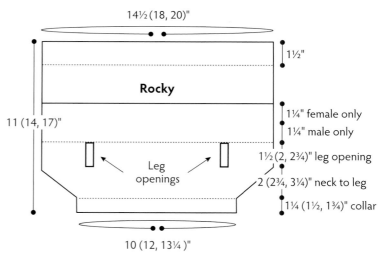

14½ (18, 20)"

Rocky

1½"

11 (14, 17)"

1¼" female only

1¼" male only

1½ (2, 2¾)" leg opening

Leg openings

2 (2¾, 3¼)" neck to leg

1¼ (1½, 1¾)" collar

10 (12, 13¼)"

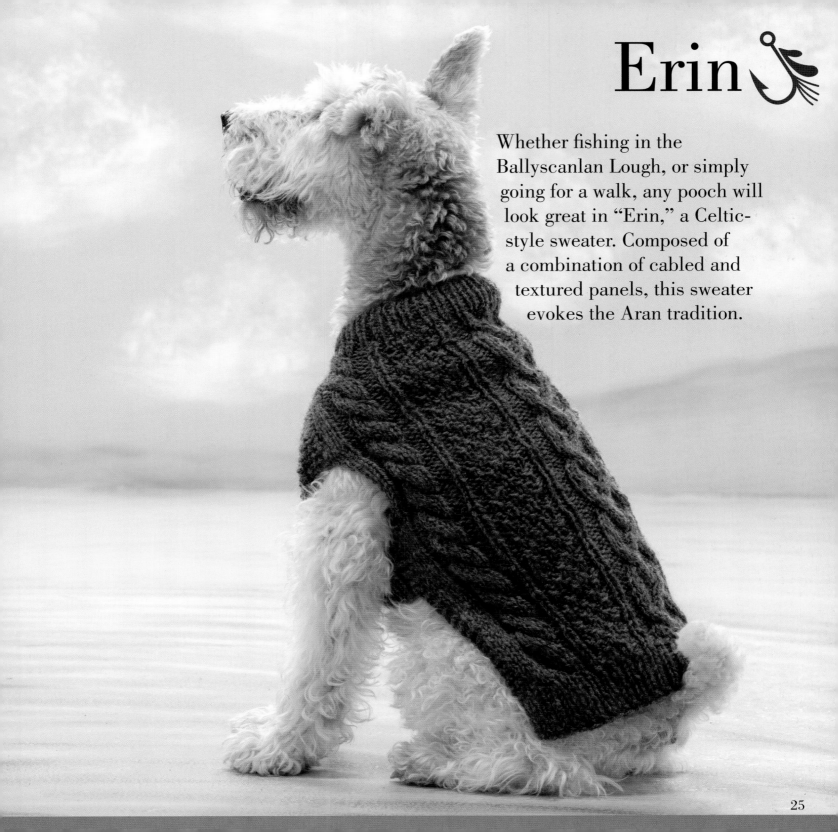

Erin

Whether fishing in the Ballyscanlan Lough, or simply going for a walk, any pooch will look great in "Erin," a Celtic-style sweater. Composed of a combination of cabled and textured panels, this sweater evokes the Aran tradition.

Skill level: Experienced ▮■■▮

Construction: Sleeveless top down

Sizes
Small (Medium, Large)

Finished Measurements
Length: 11 (14, 17)"

Neck circumference: 9¾ (11½, 13¾)"

Chest width: 4¼ (6, 6¾)"

Chest circumference: 14 (17½, 20½)"

Note: Sizes above are approximate. Slight changes in number of stitches and/or rows have been made to accommodate the stitch pattern and/or gauge. The garment will stretch. For additional sizing information, see "The Right Fit" (page 8).

Materials
1 (2, 2) skein of Wool-Ease from Lion Brand Yarn (80% acrylic, 20% wool; 85 g; 197 yds) in color Oxford Grey (4)

US size 8 (5 mm) double-pointed needles and 16" to 22" circular needle, or size needed to obtain gauge

US size 6 (4 mm) double-pointed needles and 16" to 22" circular needle

8 stitch markers in different colors

Cable needle

Tapestry needle

Gauge
18 sts and 24 rows = 4" in St st using size 8 needles

Seed Stitch (worked over an even number of sts)
Row 1: *K1, P1; rep from * to end.

Row 2: *P1, K1; rep from * to end.

Rep rows 1 and 2 for patt.

Seed Stitch (worked over an odd number of sts)
All rows: K1, *P1, K1; rep from * to end.

Pattern Stitch
See chart for size you're making (pages 27 and 28).

Collar
With smaller needles, CO 44 (52, 62) sts and distribute onto 3 dpns. Join in the round, taking care not to twist sts, and PM A to denote beg of rnd. Work in K1, P1 rib for 8 (9, 12) rnds.

Neck to Leg Opening
Change to circular needle when needed. If desired, use different-colored markers to separate each panel of Aran sts on chart.

Next rnd: Change to larger needles, sl marker A, M1L, PM B, work foundation row 1 of chart to end of rnd.

Next rnd: Sl marker A, M1L, P1, M1R, sl marker B, work foundation row 2 to end of rnd.

Next rnd: Sl marker A, M1L, *work in seed st to next marker, M1R, sl marker B, work next row of chart to end of rnd.

Rep last rnd until there are 19 (27, 31) sts between markers.

Work even for 2 (4, 4) rnds—63 (79, 93) sts. Note last row worked of chart.

Chest
Separate chest and back sts for leg openings as follows: sl marker A, work in seed st to marker B. Turn work. Leave rem sts unworked for back.

Cont to work chest sts in seed st, turning at end of each row, for 10 (12, 16) rows, ending with a RS row. Cut yarn, leaving approx 8" tail.

Back
Join working yarn to back, starting on RS row. Cont to work back sts in patt for 10 (12, 16) rows, ending with a WS row. Turn work.

Join to Work in the Round
Next rnd: Knit across back to marker A. Join back to chest, keeping marker in place, work in seed st to marker B, join chest to back, keeping marker in place, work in patt to end of rnd.

Work 5 rnds in patt.

For male dogs only, beg chest rib now. For female dogs, work 8 more rnds, and then begin chest rib.

Chest Rib

Optional: For tighter chest rib, work chest sts with smaller circular needles and back sts with larger circular needles. See "Working with Two Circular Needles at the Same Time" (page 10). In this case, markers can be removed when sts are separated on the two circular needles.

Note: Because cables tend to pull the fabric in, the gauge is tighter. Stitches are borrowed from the chest section here to add width to the back section.

Next rnd: Remove marker A, K3, PM A (marker has moved forward 3 sts), work in P1, K1 rib until 3 sts before marker B, sl next 3 sts pw onto RH needle, remove marker B, slide these 3 sts back onto LH needle, take care not to twist. PM B (marker B has moved back 3 sts), P3, work in patt to end of rnd.

Cont in patt for 8 rnds.

Remove marker A, BO 13 (21, 25) chest sts in patt, remove marker B—50 (58, 68) sts.

Complete the Back

Cont working back and forth in patt until piece measures 9½ (12½, 15½)" from bottom edge of collar rib or until jacket is 1½" shorter than desired length.

Change to smaller needles, work in K1, P1 rib for a total of 9 rows.

BO in patt.

Weave in all ends.

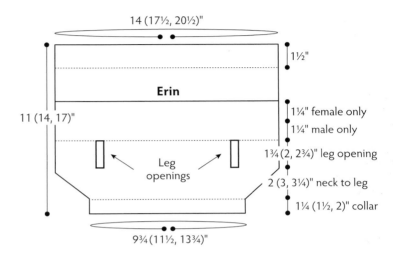

14 (17½, 20½)"

1½"

Erin

11 (14, 17)"

1¼" female only

1¼" male only

1¾ (2, 2¾)" leg opening

Leg openings

2 (3, 3¼)" neck to leg

1¼ (1½, 2)" collar

9¾ (11½, 13¾)"

Erin - Size Small

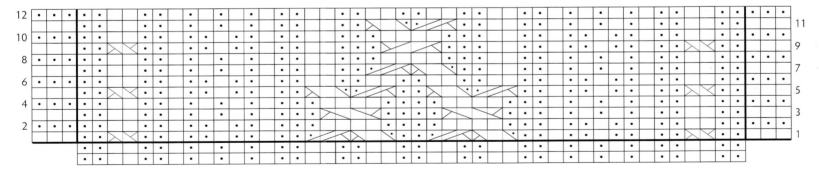

Legend

☐ K on RS, P on WS

⊡ P on RS, K on WS

Sl 2 to cn and hold in front, K2, K2 from cn

Sl 2 to cn and hold in front, P1, K2 from cn

Sl 1 to cn and hold in back, K2, P1 from cn

Sl 2 to cn and hold in back, K2, K2 from cn

Sl 1 to cn and hold in front, K1, K1 from cn

Erin - Size Medium

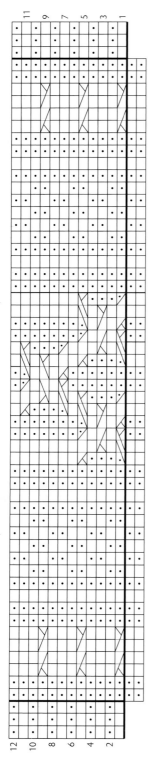

Legend

⬜	K on RS, P on WS
▪	P on RS, K on WS
	Sl 2 to cn and hold in front, K2, K2 from cn
	Sl 2 to cn and hold in front, P1, K2 from cn
	Sl 1 to cn and hold in back, K2, P1 from cn
	Sl 2 to cn and hold in back, K2, K2 from cn

Erin - Size Large

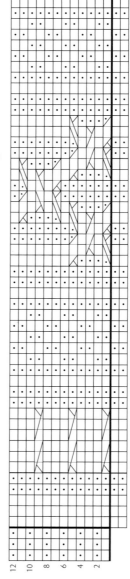

Legend

⬜	K on RS, P on WS
▪	P on RS, K on WS
	Sl 2 to cn and hold in front, K2, K2 from cn
	Sl 2 to cn and hold in front, P1, K2 from cn
	Sl 1 to cn and hold in back, K2, P1 from cn
	Sl 2 to cn and hold in back, K2, K2 from cn
	Sl 3 to cn and hold in front, K3, K3 from cn

Buddy and ♂♀ Diamond Girl

His and her sweaters from one basic pattern, "Buddy" and "Diamond Girl" use only knit and purl stitches to create these dimensionally textured fabrics, so you can choose a stitch pattern that suits your dog's personality best.

Sizes

Small (Medium, Large)

Finished Measurements

Length: 11 (14, 17)"

Neck circumference: 9 (12, 13)"

Chest width: 4¼ (5¾, 6¾)"

Chest circumference: 13½ (17¾, 19¾)"

Note: Sizes above are approximate. Slight changes in number of stitches and/or rows have been made to accommodate the stitch pattern and/or gauge. The garments will stretch. For additional sizing information, see "The Right Fit" (page 8).

Materials

1 (2, 2) skein of Vanna's Choice from Lion Brand Yarn (100% acrylic; 100 g; 170 yds) **[4]** in color Aqua for Buddy and color Pink Poodle for Diamond Girl

US size 9 (5.5 mm) double-pointed needles and 16" to 22" circular needle, or size needed to obtain gauge

US size 7 (4.5 mm) double-pointed needles and 16" to 22" circular needle

2 stitch markers in different colors

Tapestry needle

Gauge

16 sts and 22 rows = 4" in St st using size 9 needles

Pattern Stitch

See charts on page 31.

Collar

With smaller needles, CO 36 (48, 52) sts and distribute onto 3 dpns. Join in the round, taking care not to twist sts, and PM A to note beg of rnd. Work in K1, P1 rib for 6 (8, 10) rnds.

Next rnd: Sl marker A, M1L, work in patt to end of rnd—37 (49, 53) sts.

Neck to Leg Opening

Change to circular needle when needed.

Next rnd: Change to larger needles, sl marker A, M1L, PM B, work row 1 of chart to end of rnd.

Next rnd: Sl marker A, M1L, knit to marker B, M1R, sl marker B, work next row of chart to end of rnd.

Rep last rnd until there are 17 (23, 27) sts between markers.

Work even for 2 (3, 4) rnds—54 (72, 80) sts. Note last row worked of chart.

Chest

Separate chest and back sts for leg openings as follows: sl marker A, knit to marker B. Turn work. Leave rem sts unworked for back.

Cont to work chest sts back and forth in St st for 8 (10, 14) rows, ending with a RS row. Cut yarn, leaving approx 8" tail.

Back

Join working yarn to back, starting on RS row. Cont to work in patt for 8 (10, 14) rows, ending with a WS row. Turn work.

Join to Work in the Round

Next rnd: Work in patt across back to marker A. Join back to chest, keeping marker in place, knit to marker B, join chest to back, keeping marker in place, work in patt to end of rnd.

Work 5 rnds in patt.

For male dogs only, beg chest rib now. For female dogs, work 7 more rnds, and then begin chest rib.

Chest Rib

Optional: For a tighter chest rib, work chest sts with smaller circular needles and back sts with larger circular needles. See "Working with Two Circular Needles at the Same Time" (page 10). In this case, markers can be removed when sts are separated on the two circular needles.

Next rnd: Sl marker A, work in P1, K1 rib (beg and end with purl), sl marker B, work in patt to end of rnd.

Rep for 6 more rnds. Remove marker A. BO 17 (23, 27) chest sts in patt. Remove marker B—37 (49, 53) sts.

Complete the Back

Cont working back and forth in patt until piece measures 9½ (12½, 15½)" from bottom edge of collar rib, or until sweater is 1½" shorter than desired length.

Change to smaller needles, work in K1, P1 rib for a total of 8 rows.

BO in patt.

Weave in all ends.

Buddy

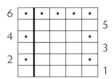

Legend

☐	K on RS, P on WS
⊡	P on RS, K on WS

Diamond Girl

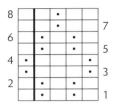

Legend

☐	K on RS, P on WS
⊡	P on RS, K on WS

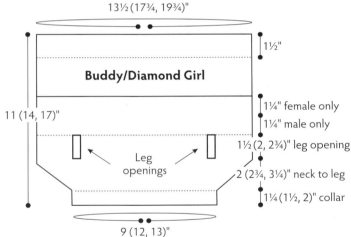

13½ (17¾, 19¾)"

1½"

Buddy/Diamond Girl

11 (14, 17)"

1¼" female only
1¼" male only
1½ (2, 2¾)" leg opening
2 (2¾, 3¼)" neck to leg
1¼ (1½, 2)" collar

Leg openings

9 (12, 13)"

Rosco

When wearing "Rosco," any dog will be ready to round 'em up in this rope-twist textured sweater. With no cable needle required, the mini cables work up easily and exhibit a fantastic textural effect.

Skill level: Intermediate ●■■◖

Construction: Sleeveless top down

Sizes
Small (Medium, Large)

Finished Measurements
Length: 11 (14, 17)"

Neck circumference: 9½ (12½, 14)"

Chest width: 4¼ (5¾, 6¾)"

Chest circumference: 13¾ (18¼, 20¾)"

Note: Sizes above are approximate. Slight changes in number of stitches and/or rows have been made to accommodate the stitch pattern and/or gauge. The garment will stretch. For additional sizing information, see "The Right Fit" (page 8).

Materials
1 (2, 2) skein of Vanna's Choice from Lion Brand Yarn (100% acrylic; 100 g; 170 yds) in color Fern ◖4◗

US size 9 (5.5 mm) double-pointed needles and 16" to 22" circular needle, or size needed to obtain gauge

US size 7 (4.5 mm) double-pointed needles and 16" to 22" circular needle

2 stitch markers in different colors

Tapestry needle

Gauge
16 sts and 22 rows = 4" in patt st using size 9 needles, slightly stretched

Special Technique
T2R (twist 2 right): Knit second st on left needle, do not remove. Knit first st on left needle, remove both sts from left needle.

Pattern Stitch
See chart on page 34.

Collar
With smaller needles, CO 38 (50, 56) sts and distribute onto 3 dpns. Join in the round, taking care not to twist sts, and PM A to note beg of rnd. Work in K1, P1 rib for 7 (9, 11) rnds.

Neck to Leg Opening
Note: Change to circular needle when needed.

Next rnd: Change to larger needles, sl marker A, M1L, PM B, work row 1 of chart to end of rnd.

Next rnd: Sl marker A, M1L, knit to marker B, M1R, sl marker B, work next row of chart to end of rnd.

Rep last rnd until there are 17 (23, 27) sts between markers—55 (73, 83) sts.

Work even for 1 (2, 2) rnds, ending with row 2 of chart.

Chest
Separate chest and back sts for leg openings as follows: sl marker A, knit to marker B. Turn work. Leave rem sts unworked for back.

Cont to work chest sts in St st, turning at end of each row, for 8 (10, 14) rows, ending with a RS row. Cut yarn, leaving approx 8" tail.

"Rosco" in alternate colorway, Mustard

Back
Join working yarn to back, starting on RS row. Cont to work back sts in patt for 8 (10, 14) rows, ending with a WS row. Turn work.

Join to Work in the Round
Next rnd: Work in patt across back to marker A. Join back to chest, keeping marker in place, knit to marker B, join chest to back, keeping marker in place, work in patt to end of rnd.

Work 1 (3, 5) rnd in patt.

For male dogs only, beg chest rib now. For female dogs, work 8 more rnds, and then begin chest rib.

Rosco

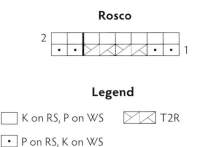

Legend

☐ K on RS, P on WS	⬛ T2R
⊡ P on RS, K on WS	

Chest Rib

Optional: For a tighter chest rib, work chest sts with smaller circular needles and back sts with larger circular needles. See "Working with Two Circular Needles at the Same Time" (page 10). In this case, markers can be removed when sts are separated on the two circular needles.

Next rnd: Sl marker A, work in P1, K1 rib (beg and end with purl), sl marker B, work in patt to end of rnd.

Rep for 6 more rnds. Remove marker A. BO 17 (23, 27) chest sts in patt. Remove marker B.

Complete the Back

Cont working back and forth in patt until piece measures 9½ (12½, 15½)" from bottom edge of collar rib or until sweater is 1½" shorter than desired length.

Change to smaller needles, work in K1, P1 rib for a total of 8 rows.

BO in patt.

Weave in all ends.

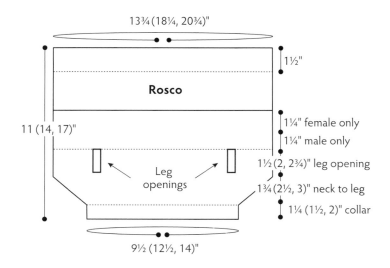

13¾ (18¼, 20¾)"

1½"

Rosco

11 (14, 17)"

1¼" female only

1¼" male only

Leg openings

1½ (2, 2¾)" leg opening

1¾ (2½, 3)" neck to leg

1¼ (1½, 2)" collar

9½ (12½, 14)"

Skye

"Skye" is a snuggly brioche-styled rib perfect for keeping the chill away. Slightly simplified from the traditional version, this brioche pattern is super easy to create using only knit, purl, and slipped stitches.

Skill level: Easy ●■□□

Construction: Sleeveless top down

Sizes

Small (Medium, Large)

Finished Measurements

Length: 11 (14, 17)"

Neck circumference: 9¼ (12, 13¼)"

Chest width: 3¾ (5½, 6½)"

Chest circumference: 13 (17½, 19¾)"

Note: Sizes above are approximate. Slight changes in number of stitches and/or rows have been made to accommodate the stitch pattern and/or gauge. The garment will stretch. For additional sizing information, see "The Right Fit" (page 8).

Materials

1 (2, 2) skein of Martha Stewart Crafts extra soft wool blend from Lion Brand Yarn (65% acrylic, 35% wool; 100 g; 164 yds) in color Winter Sky (**4**)

US size 7 (4.5 mm) double-pointed needles and 16" to 22" circular needle, or size needed to obtain gauge

US size 5 (3.75 mm) double-pointed needles and 16" to 22" circular needle

2 stitch markers in different colors

Tapestry needle

Gauge

18 sts and 25 rows = 4" in St st using size 7 needles

Pattern Stitch

See chart on page 37.

Collar

With smaller needles, CO 42 (54, 60) sts and distribute onto 3 dpns. Join in the round, taking care not to twist sts, and PM A to note beg of rnd. Work in K1, P1 rib 6 (8, 11) rnds.

Next rnd: Inc 1 (1, 3) st evenly—43 (55, 63) sts.

Neck to Leg Opening

Change to circular needle when needed.

Next rnd: Change to larger needles, sl marker A, M1L, PM B, work row 1 of chart to end of rnd.

Next rnd: Sl marker A, M1L, knit to marker B, M1R, sl marker B, work next row of chart to end of rnd.

Rep last rnd until there are 17 (25, 29) sts between markers—60 (80, 92) sts.

Work even for 1 (3, 5) rnd, ending with row 2 of chart.

Chest

Separate chest and back sts for leg openings as follows: sl marker A, knit to marker B. Turn work. Leave rem sts unworked for back.

Cont to work chest sts in St st, turning at end of each row, for 10 (12, 16) rows, ending with a RS row. Cut yarn, leaving approx 8" tail.

Back

Join working yarn to back, starting on RS row. Cont to work back sts in patt for 10 (12, 16) rows, ending with a WS row. Turn work.

Join to Work in the Round

Next rnd: Work in patt across back to marker A. Join back to chest, keeping marker in place, knit to marker B, join chest to back, keeping marker in place, work in patt to end of rnd.

Work 5 rnds in patt.

For male dogs only, beg chest rib now. For female dogs, work 8 more rnds, and then begin chest rib.

Chest Rib

Optional: For a tighter chest rib, work chest sts with smaller circular needles and back sts with larger circular needles. See "Working with Two Circular Needles at the Same Time" (page 10). In this case, markers can be removed when sts are separated on the two circular needles.

Next rnd: Sl marker A, work in P1, K1 rib (beg and end with purl), sl marker B, work in patt to end of rnd.

Rep for 8 more rnds. Remove marker A. BO 17 (25, 29) chest sts in patt. Remove marker B—43 (55, 63) sts.

Complete the Back

Cont working back and forth in patt until piece measures 9½ (12½, 15½)" from bottom edge of collar rib or until sweater is 1½" shorter than desired length.

Change to smaller needles, work in K1, P1 rib for a total of 9 rows.

BO in patt.

Weave in all ends.

Skye

Legend

☐ K on RS, P on WS

• P on RS, K on WS

⩑ Sl 1 with yarn at WS of work

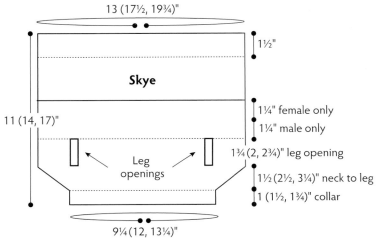

13 (17½, 19¾)"

1½"

Skye

11 (14, 17)"

1¼" female only

1¼" male only

1¾ (2, 2¾)" leg opening

Leg openings

1½ (2½, 3¼)" neck to leg

1 (1½, 1¾)" collar

9¼ (12, 13¼)"

# Max

"Max" is perfect to wear for fetching candy at Halloween or a ball in the park. For year-round wear, eliminate the leaves for a two-color wide-rib sweater, or change the look completely by purling the knit stitches and knitting the purl stitches in the rib.

Construction: Sleeveless top down

Sizes

Small (Medium, Large)

Finished Measurements

Length: 11 (14, 17)"

Neck circumference: 9¾ (11¾, 13¼)"

Chest width: 4½ (5¾, 6¾)"

Chest circumference: 14¼ (17½, 20)"

Note: Sizes above are approximate. Slight changes in number of stitches and/or rows have been made to accommodate the stitch pattern and/or gauge. The garment will stretch. For additional sizing information, see "The Right Fit" (page 8).

Materials

Heartland from Lion Brand Yarn (100% acrylic; 142 g; 251 yds) (4)

MC 1 (1, 2) skein in color Yosemite

CC 1 (1, 1) skein in color Kings Canyon

US size 8 (5 mm) double-pointed needles and 16" to 22" circular needle, or size needed to obtain gauge

US size 6 (4 mm) double-pointed needles and 16" to 22" circular needle

2 stitch markers in different colors and 1 safety pin–style stitch marker

Tapestry needle

Gauge

17 sts and 24 rows = 4" in St st using size 8 needles

Collar

With smaller needles and CC, CO 42 (50, 56) sts and distribute onto 3 dpns. Join in the round, taking care not to twist sts, and PM A to denote beg of rnd. Work in K1, P1 rib for 7 (9, 11) rnds.

Next rnd: Purl to last 2 sts; for size Small, M1, P2; for sizes Medium and Large, P2tog—43 (49, 55) sts.

Place safety pin marker on last stitch of rnd. This marker will stay in place to help locate sts to pick up for leaves on collar. Cut yarn, leaving approx 8" tail.

Neck to Leg Opening

Change to circular needle when needed.

Next rnd: Change to larger needles and MC, sl marker A, M1L, PM B, [P1, K6 (7, 8)] 6 times, P1.

Next rnd: Sl marker A, M1L, knit to marker B, M1R, sl marker B. Work in patt to end of rnd.

Rep last rnd until there are 19 (25, 29) sts between markers.

Work even for 2 (4, 5) rnds—62 (74, 84) sts.

Chest

Separate chest and back sts for leg openings as follows: sl marker A, knit to marker B. Turn work. Leave rem sts unworked for back.

Cont to work chest sts in St st, turning at end of each row, for 8 (10, 16) rows, ending with a RS row. Cut yarn, leaving approx 8" tail.

Back

Join working yarn to back, starting on RS row. Cont to work back sts in patt for 8 (10, 16) rows, ending with a WS row. Turn work.

Join to Work in the Round

Next rnd: Work in patt across back to marker A. Join back to chest, keeping marker in place, knit to marker B, join chest to back, keeping marker in place, work in patt to end of rnd.

Work 5 rnds in patt.

For male dogs only, beg chest rib now. For female dogs, work 8 more rnds, and then begin chest rib.

Chest Rib

Optional: For tighter chest rib, work chest sts with smaller circular needles and back sts with larger circular needles. See

"Max," without leaves, in alternate colorway, Olympic and Yellowstone

"Working with Two Circular Needles at the Same Time" (page 10). In this case, markers can be removed when sts are separated on the two circular needles.

Next rnd: Sl marker A, work in K1, P1 rib (beg and end with knit), sl marker B, work in patt to end of rnd.

Rep for 7 more rnds. Remove marker A. BO 19 (25, 29) chest sts in patt. Remove marker B—43 (49, 55) sts.

Complete the Back

Cont working back and forth in patt until piece measures 9½ (12½, 15½)" from bottom edge of collar rib, or until sweater is 1½" shorter than desired length.

Change to CC and smaller needles and work in K1, P1 rib for a total of 9 rows.

BO in patt.

Weave in all ends.

Leafy Collar

There are 6 wide-ribbed sections in the sweater back; each leaf will be worked across 2 sections.

Beg with first knit st of first wide-ribbed section (next to st marked with safety pin), PU 13 (15, 17) sts. Turn work.

Row 1: Sl first st pw, purl to end of row.

Row 2: Sl first st kw, K2tog, knit until 3 sts rem, ssk, K1 (2 sts dec).

Rep last 2 rows until 5 sts rem.

Next row: Sl first st pw, purl to end of row. Turn work.

Next row: K2tog, K1, K2tog. Turn work—3 sts.

Next row: P3, turn work.

Next row: K3tog. Cut yarn, leaving approx 8" tail and pull through loop.

Holding leaf against the sweater, pull yarn end through the fabric to the inside and secure loosely.

Weave in all ends.

Rep instructions above for rem 2 leaves, skipping a purl st between each leaf, beg next leaf at first knit st of next wide rib.

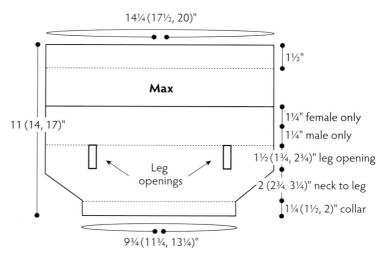

14¼ (17½, 20)"

1½"

Max

11 (14, 17)"

1¼" female only

1¼" male only

1½ (1¾, 2¾)" leg opening

Leg openings

2 (2¾, 3¼)" neck to leg

1¼ (1½, 2)" collar

9¾ (11¾, 13¼)"

Tiffany

Can you tell how divinely happy this pup is . . . when she's dressed up? Strands of pearls add a touch of class, or you can eliminate them for a more casual look. The ribbed section keeps the dress from hanging too low.

Threading Beads on Yarn

Thread sewing needle with 10"-long piece of thread. Bring both ends together and tie a small knot, making a loop. Place end of working yarn into this loop with about 3" to 4" of yarn through the loop, and let hang. Use sewing needle to thread necessary number of beads over thread and slide onto yarn.

String Beads

String 25 (64, 108) 6 mm pearl beads.

Collar

CO 50 (64, 72) sts and distribute onto 3 dpns. Join in the round, taking care not to twist sts, and PM A to note beg of rnd. Work in K1, P1 rib for 3 rnds.

Next rnd: With yarn in front, sl knit st pw and slide a bead close to first stitch on RH needle, P1. Continue to sl 1, slide bead, P1 in this manner to end of rnd.

Next 2 rnds: Work in K1, P1 rib.

Rep last 3 rnds 0 (1, 2) more times.

Knit next rnd.

Neck to Leg Opening

Change to circular needle when needed.

Next rnd: Sl marker A, M1L, PM B, knit to end of rnd.

Next rnd: Sl marker A, M1L, knit to marker B, M1R, sl marker B. Knit to end of rnd.

Rep last rnd until there are 23 (31, 37) sts between markers.

Work even for 3 (4, 5) rnds—73 (95, 109) sts.

Chest

Separate chest and back sts for leg openings as follows: sl marker A, knit to marker B. Turn work. Leave rem sts unworked for back.

Cont to work chest sts in St st, turning at end of each row, for 12 (16, 20) rows, ending with a RS row. Cut yarn, leaving approx 8" tail.

Back

Join working yarn to back, starting on RS row. Cont to work back sts in St st for 12 (16, 20) rows, ending with a WS row. Turn work.

"Tiffany," without pearls, in alternate colorway, Bronze

Join to Work in the Round

Next rnd: Knit across back to marker A. Join back to chest, keeping marker in place, knit to marker B, join chest to back, keeping marker in place, work in St st to end of rnd.

Work 12 (15, 20) rnds in patt.

Tummy Rib

Optional: For a tighter tummy rib, work tummy sts with smaller circular needles and back sts with larger circular needles. See "Working with Two Circular Needles at the Same Time" (page 10). In this case, markers can be removed when sts are separated on the two circular needles.

Next rnd: Sl marker A, work in P1, K1 rib to marker B, knit to end of rnd.

Rep last rnd 18 (24, 30) times.

Ruffle

Next rnd: Work in patt to marker B, (K1, M1R) to end of rnd—146 (190, 218) sts.

Next rnd: Work in patt to marker B, purl to end of rnd.

Next rnd: Work in patt to marker B, knit to end of rnd.

Rep last 2 rnds 2 times.

BO in patt.

Weave in all ends.

The number of rows of pearls is dependent on the size you're making. "Tiffany," shown here in size medium, has two rows of pearls; size small has only one row. You can choose to add more rows if you desire.

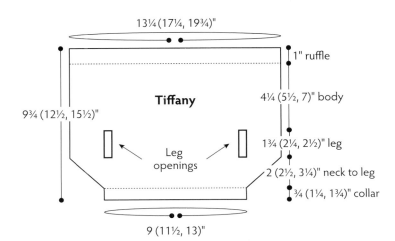

13¼ (17¼, 19¾)"

1" ruffle

4¼ (5½, 7)" body

Tiffany

9¾ (12½, 15½)"

Leg openings

1¾ (2¼, 2½)" leg

2 (2½, 3¼)" neck to leg

¾ (1¼, 1¾)" collar

9 (11½, 13)"

Cecil

Slow and steady may win the race, but this long-sleeved turtleneck is so quick to knit, you'll be crossing the finish line before you know it.

Skill level: Intermediate ●■■◻

Construction: Top down with raglan sleeves

About Raglan Construction: The top-down construction for the raglan-sleeve style works a yoke that includes the shoulder part of the sleeve. Designed specifically to fit the angle of a dog's front legs, the increases for the sleeves are not the same as for the chest and back. While the main sweater is completed, the sleeve stitches are held on waste yarn to be worked later.

Sizes
Small (Medium, Large)

Finished Measurements

Length: 11 (14, 17)"

Neck circumference: 8¾ (11, 13¼)"

Chest width: 5 (6¼, 7¾)"

Chest circumference: 14¼ (18¾, 22½)"

Note: Sizes above are approximate. Slight changes in number of stitches and/or rows have been made to accommodate the stitch pattern and/or gauge. The garment will stretch. For additional sizing information, see "The Right Fit" (page 8).

Materials
1 (2, 2) skein of Tweed Stripes from Lion Brand Yarn (100% acrylic; 85 g; 144 yds) in color Caribbean 🧶5

US size 10 (6 mm) double-pointed needles and 16" to 22" circular needle, or size needed to obtain gauge

US size 8 (5 mm) double-pointed needles and 16" to 22" circular needle

US size 11 (8 mm) double-pointed needles (for turtleneck option only)

"Cecil" crewneck in alternate colorway, Purple Mist

4 stitch markers in different colors

Tapestry needle

Gauge
14½ sts and 18 rows = 4" in St st using size 10 needles

Turtleneck *Only*
With size 11 needles, CO 32 (40, 48) sts and distribute onto 3 dpns. Join in the round, taking care not to twist sts, and PM A to note beg of rnd.

Work in K2, P2 rib for 8 (9, 10) rnds. Change to size 8 needles, and continue in patt for an additional 7 (8, 9) rnds. Skip to "Yoke" section, right.

Crewneck *Only*
With size 8 needles, CO 32 (40, 48) sts and distribute onto 3 dpns. Join in the round, taking care not to twist sts, and PM A to note beg of rnd. Work in K2, P2 rib 7 (8, 9) rnds.

Yoke
Change to circular needle when needed.

Set-up rnd: Sl marker A, (beg of rnd AND start of right sleeve), work 5 (6, 8) sts, PM

B (beg of chest sts), work 6 (7, 8) sts, PM C (beg of left sleeve), work 5 (6, 8) sts, PM D (beg of back sts), work 16 (21, 24) sts to end of rnd. Rnd beg at back edge of right sleeve, working right sleeve, chest, left sleeve, and back in that order.

Change to size 10 needles.

Rnd 1: Sl marker A, knit to next marker, sl marker B, K1, M1L, knit to 1 st before marker, M1R, K1, sl marker C, knit to next marker, sl marker D, K1, M1L, knit to 1 st before end of rnd, M1R, K1 (2 inc chest, 2 inc back).

Rnd 2: Knit.

Rnd 3: Sl marker A, knit to 1 st before marker, M1R, K1, sl marker B, knit to next marker, sl marker C, K1, M1L, knit to next marker, sl marker D, K1, M1L, knit to 1 st before end of rnd, M1R, K1 (1 inc RH sleeve, 2 inc back, 1 inc LH sleeve).

Rnd 4: Knit.

Rnd 5: *Sl marker, K1, M1L, knit to 1 stitch before marker, M1R, K1; rep from * to end of rnd (2 inc RH sleeve, 2 inc chest, 2 inc back, 2 inc LH sleeve).

Rep last 5 rnds 2 (3, 4) times more—80 (104, 128) sts divided as follows: 14 (18, 23) sts each sleeve; 18 (23, 28) sts chest; 34 (45, 54) sts back.

Separate Sleeves and Body

Next rnd: Sl marker A, sl 14 (18, 23) sleeve sts to waste yarn, remove marker B, knit to marker C, sl 14 (18, 23) sleeve sts to waste yarn, sl marker D, knit to end of rnd.

Knit 2 rnds—53 (68, 82) sts.

For male dogs only, beg chest rib now. For female dogs, work 6 more rnds, and then begin chest rib.

Chest Rib

Optional: For a tighter chest rib, work chest sts with smaller circular needles and back sts with larger circular needles. See "Working with Two Circular Needles at the Same Time" (page 10). In this case, markers can be removed when sts are separated on the two circular needles.

Next rnd: Sl marker A, work in P1, K1 rib to last 2 sts before marker D, P2tog, knit to end of rnd.

Work in patt for 5 more rnds. Remove marker A. BO 18 (23, 28) chest sts in patt. Remove marker D—34 (45, 54) sts.

Complete the Back

Cont working back and forth in patt until piece measures 9½ (12½, 15½)" from bottom edge of collar rib or until sweater is 1½" shorter than desired length.

Medium size only

Decrease 1 stitch in last row before beginning rib—34 (44, 54) sts.

All sizes

Change to size 8 needles, work in K2, P2 rib for a total of 7 rows.

BO in patt.

Weave in all ends.

Sleeves

Place 14 (18, 23) held sleeve sts on size 10 needles, join working yarn, and PU and knit 2 (2, 1) sts at underarm, PM and join in the round—16 (20, 24) sts.

Knit even for 2 (3, 4)". Change to smaller needles. Work in K2, P2 rib for 5 rnds.

BO in patt.

Rep for second sleeve.

Remove waste yarn.

Weave in all ends.

14¼ (18¾, 22½)"

11 (14, 17)"

WS of back

1½"

1¼" female only

1¼" male only

2 (3, 4)"

Cecil

3¼ (4½, 5½)"

1½ (1¾, 2)" collar

8¾ (11, 13¼)"

Waldo

Where's Waldo? Whatever your puppy's name, he'll be easy to spot in this striped sweater fashioned after the favorite book character's attire! Add stars to the blue background for a patriotic look, or work stripes all the way to the bottom for the holidays.

US size 9 (5.5 mm) double-pointed needles and 16" to 22" circular needle, or size needed to obtain gauge

US size 7 (4.5 mm) double-pointed needles and 16" to 22" circular needle

4 stitch markers in different colors

Waste yarn

Tapestry needle

Gauge

16 sts and 22 rows = 4" in St st using size 9 needles

Collar

Alternate 2 rnds of MC and 2 rnds of CC1 throughout unless otherwise indicated. With smaller needles and MC, CO 36 (48, 54) sts and distribute onto 3 dpns. Join in the round, taking care not to twist sts, and PM A to denote beg of rnd. Work in K1, P1 rib for 6 (8, 12) rnds.

Yoke

Change to circular needle when needed.

Set-up rnd: Sl marker A (beg of rnd AND start of right sleeve), work 6 (8, 9) sts, PM B (beg of chest sts), work 6 (8, 9) sts, PM C (beg of left sleeve), work 6 (8, 9) sts, PM D (beg of back sts), work 18 (24, 27) sts to end of rnd. Rnd beg at back edge of right sleeve, working right sleeve, chest, left sleeve, and back in that order.

Change to larger needles.

Rnd 1: Sl marker A, knit to next marker, sl marker B, K1, M1L, knit to 1 st before marker, M1R, K1, sl marker C, knit to next marker, sl marker D, K1, M1L, knit to 1 st before end of rnd, M1R, K1 (2 inc chest, 1 inc back).

Rnd 2: Knit.

Rnd 3: Sl marker A, knit to 1 st before marker, M1R, K1, sl marker B, knit to next marker, sl marker C, K1, M1L, knit to next marker, sl marker D, K1, M1L, knit to 1 st before end of rnd, M1R, K1 (1 inc RH sleeve, 1 inc LH sleeve, 2 inc back).

Rnd 4: Knit.

Rnd 5: *Sl marker, K1, M1L, knit to 1 stitch before marker, M1R, K1; rep from * to end of rnd (2 inc RH sleeve, 2 inc chest, 2 inc LH sleeve, 2 inc back).

Rnd 6: Knit.

Rep last 6 rnds 2 (3, 4) times more—84 (112, 134) sts divided as follows: 15 (20, 24) sts each sleeve; 18 (24, 29) sts chest; 36 (48, 57) sts back.

Separate Sleeves and Body

Next rnd: Sl marker A, sl 15 (20, 24) sleeve sts to waste yarn, remove marker B, knit to marker C, sl 15 (20, 24) sleeve sts to waste yarn, sl marker D, knit to end of rnd.

Knit 2 rnds—54 (72, 86) sts.

For male dogs only, beg chest rib now. For female dogs, switch to CC2 and work 6 more rnds, and then begin chest rib.

Chest Rib

Optional: For a tighter chest rib, work chest sts with smaller circular needles and back sts with larger circular needles. See "Working with Two Circular Needles at the Same Time" (page 10). In this case, markers can be removed when sts are separated on the two circular needles.

Next rnd: With CC2, sl marker A, work in P1, K1 rib to last 2 sts before marker D, P2tog, knit to end of rnd.

Work even for 4 more rnds. Remove marker A. BO 18 (24, 29) chest sts in patt. Remove marker D—36 (48, 57) sts.

Complete the Back

With CC2, cont working back and forth in patt until piece measures 9½ (12½, 15½)" from bottom edge of collar rib, or until sweater is 1½" shorter than desired length.

Change to smaller needles, work in K1, P1 rib for a total of 8 rows.

BO in patt.

Weave in all ends.

Sleeves

Place 15 (20, 24) held sleeve sts on larger needles, join working yarn and PU 1 (2, 2) st at underarm, PM and join in the round—17 (22, 26) sts.

Knit, alternating MC and CC1 every 2 rnds, for a total of 12 (16, 20) rnds. Change to smaller needles. Work in K1, P1 rib for 5 rnds.

BO in patt.

Rep for second sleeve.

Remove waste yarns.

Weave in all ends.

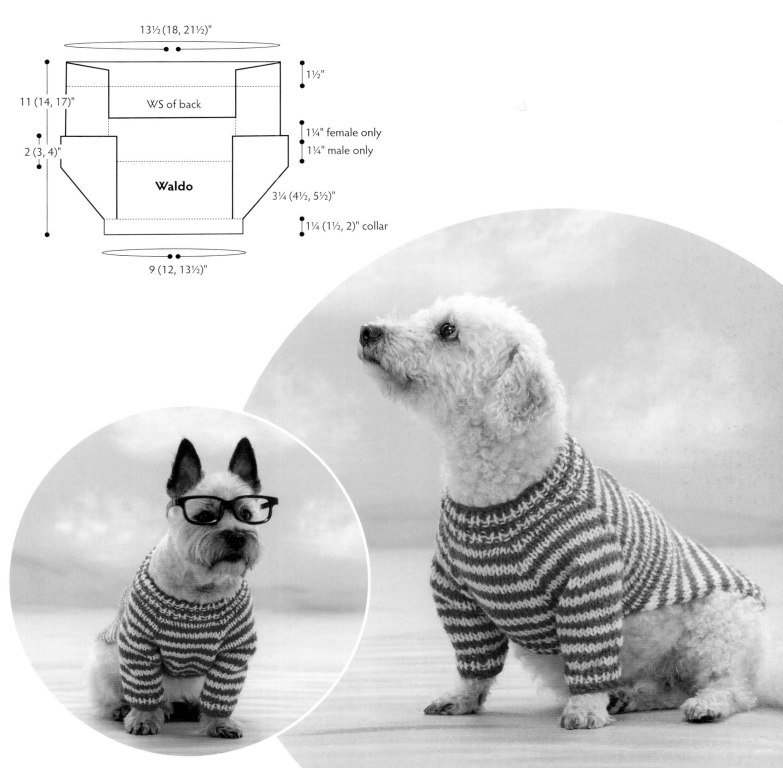

13½ (18, 21½)"

1½"

11 (14, 17)"

WS of back

1¼" female only

1¼" male only

2 (3, 4)"

Waldo

3¼ (4½, 5½)"

1¼ (1½, 2)" collar

9 (12, 13½)"

Taffy

Any dog will be ready to go to the garden party of the season in "Taffy," a short-sleeved sweater. Extra increases and decreases give dimension to the sleeves, creating the puffy look.

Skill level: Intermediate ●■■◖

Construction: Top down with raglan sleeves

About Raglan Construction: The top-down construction for the raglan-sleeve style works a yoke that includes the shoulder part of the sleeve. Designed specifically to fit the angle of a dog's front legs, the increases for the sleeves are not the same as the chest and back. While the main sweater is completed, the sleeve stitches are held on waste yarn to be worked later.

Sizes
Small (Medium, Large)

Finished Measurements
Length: 11 (14, 17)"

Neck circumference: 9 (11, 13)"

Chest width: 5½ (6½, 7½)"

Chest circumference: 14½ (17½, 20½)"

Note: Sizes above are approximate. Slight changes in number of stitches and/or rows have been made to accommodate the stitch pattern and/or gauge. The garment will stretch. For additional sizing information, see "The Right Fit" (page 8).

Materials
2 (3, 4) skeins of Jamie from Lion Brand Yarn (100% acrylic; 50 g; 137 yds) in color Peachy (3)

US size 6 (4 mm) double-pointed needles and 16" to 22" circular needle, or size needed to obtain gauge

US size 4 (3.5 mm) double-pointed needles and 16" to 22" circular needle

4 stitch markers in different colors

Waste yarn

Tapestry needle

Gauge
21 sts and 29 rows = 4" in St st using size 6 needles

Pattern Stitch
See chart on page 54.

Collar
With smaller needles, CO 48 (58, 68) sts and distribute onto 3 dpns. Join in the round, taking care not to twist sts, and PM A to denote beg of rnd.

Work in K1, P1 rib 9 (11, 13) rnds.

Yoke
Change to circular needle when needed.

Set-up rnd: Sl marker A (beg of rnd AND start of right sleeve), work 8 (9, 11) sts, PM B (beg of chest sts), work 8 (10, 12) sts, PM C (beg of left sleeve), work 8 (9, 11) sts, PM D (beg of back sts), work 24 (30, 34) sts to end of rnd. Rnd beg at back edge of right sleeve, working right sleeve, chest, left sleeve, and back in that order.

Change to larger needles. Beg chart, starting with rnd 1. *Note:* St patt is used for back section only. Sleeves and chest are worked in St st.

Rnd 1: Sl marker, K1, YO, work in patt to 1 st before next marker, YO, K1; rep from * to end of rnd (2 inc RH sleeve, 2 inc chest, 2 inc LH sleeve, 2 inc back).

Rnd 2: Work even in patt.

Raglan shaping with yarn overs creates an attractive, lacy look for the sleeve.

Rnd 3: Sl marker A, work in patt to 1 st before marker, YO, K1, sl marker B, work in patt to next marker, sl marker C, K1, YO, work in patt to next marker, sl marker D, K1, YO, work in patt to 1 st before end of rnd, YO, K1 (1 inc RH sleeve, 1 inc LH sleeve, 2 inc back).

Rnd 4: Work even in patt.

Rnd 5: *Sl marker, K1, YO, work in patt to 1 stitch before marker, YO, K1; rep from * to end of rnd. (2 inc RH sleeve, 2 inc chest, 2 inc LH sleeve, 2 inc back).

Rnd 6: Work even in patt.

Rep last 6 rnds 4 (5, 6) times more—148 (178, 208) sts divided as follows: 33 (39, 46) sts *each* sleeve; 28 (34, 40) sts chest; 54 (66, 76) sts back.

Separate Sleeves and Body

Sl marker A, sl 33 (39, 46) sleeve sts to waste yarn, remove marker B, work in patt to marker C, sl 33 (39, 46) sleeve sts to waste yarn, sl marker D, work in patt to end of rnd—82 (100, 116) sts.

Work in patt for 14 (16, 18) rnds. Begin chest rib.

Chest Rib

Optional: For a tighter chest rib, work chest sts with smaller circular needles and back sts with larger circular needles. See "Working with Two Circular Needles at the Same Time" (page 10). In this case, markers can be removed when sts are separated on the two circular needles.

Next rnd: Sl marker A, work in P1, K1 rib to last 2 sts before marker D, P2tog, work in patt to end of rnd.

Work even for 8 more rnds. Remove marker A. BO 28 (34, 40) chest sts in patt. Remove marker D—54 (66, 76) sts.

Complete the Back

Cont working back and forth in patt until piece measures 9½ (12½, 15½)" from bottom edge of collar rib, or until sweater is 1½" shorter than desired length.

Change to smaller needles, work in K1, P1 rib for a total of 11 rows.

BO in patt.

Weave in all ends.

Sleeves

Place 33 (39, 46) held sleeve sts on larger needles, join working yarn and PU 2 sts at underarm, PM and join in the round—35 (41, 48) sts.

Next rnd: *K2tog, K3; rep from * around, knitting rem 0 (1, 3) sts—28 (34, 42) sts.

Change to smaller needles. Work in K1, P1 rib for 7 rnds.

BO in patt.

Rep for second sleeve.

Remove waste yarn.

Weave in all ends.

Taffy

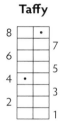

Legend

☐ K on RS, P on WS

⊡ P on RS, K on WS

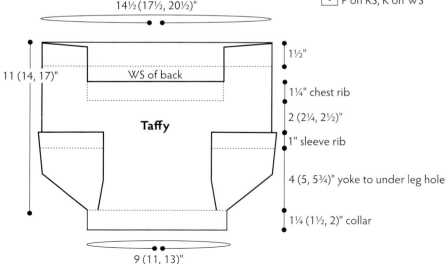

14½ (17½, 20½)"

11 (14, 17)"

WS of back

Taffy

9 (11, 13)"

1½"

1¼" chest rib

2 (2¼, 2½)"

1" sleeve rib

4 (5, 5¾)" yoke to under leg hole

1¼ (1½, 2)" collar

Buttercup

Your dog will be as pretty
as a flower in this lovely
lace dress. This piece is
worked from the bottom
up to allow for a sweet
scalloped edge that can
only be worked from
the cast on.

Pattern Note

This is designed to be a short, close-fitting dress that will stretch to fit around the dog's chest and tummy. If necessary, you can add length before beginning the leg opening. For a looser fit, work the next size larger. I've included an Extra-Large size to accommodate a looser fit for larger dogs. For size Small, use double-pointed needles throughout.

Lower Edge

With larger circular needle, CO 72 (84, 96, 108) sts. Join in the round, taking care not to twist sts, and PM A to note beg of rnd.

Rnd 1: Knit.

Rnd 2: Purl.

Beg chart starting with row 1, and work even for 24 (34, 40, 48) rnds, ending with rnd 2. Piece measures approx 4¼ (6, 7, 8¼)".

From marker A, count 49 (55, 61, 67) sts and PM B.

Back

Separate chest and back sts for leg openings as follows: sl marker A, work in patt to marker B. Turn work. Leave rem sts unworked for chest.

Cont to work back sts in patt, turning at end of each row, for 12 (14, 16, 18) rows, ending with row 1. Cut yarn, leaving approx 8" tail.

Chest

Join yarn to chest sts, RS facing you, and K23 (29, 35, 41) sts to end of row. Turn work. Work in St st for 10 (12, 14, 16) rows, ending with a RS row.

Leg Opening to Neck

Change to dpns when needed.

Next rnd: Sl marker A, join chest to back and work across back sts in patt, join back to chest, PM B, knit to end of rnd.

Next rnd: Sl marker A, work in patt to marker B, sl marker B, ssk, knit to last 2 sts, K2tog (2 sts dec).

Rep last rnd until there are 3 (3, 3, 3) sts between markers.

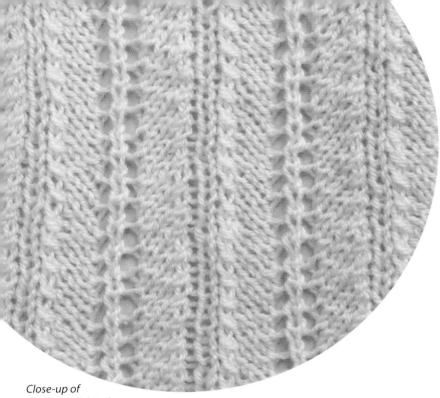

Close-up of "Buttercup" detail

Next rnd: Sl marker A, work in patt to marker B, sl marker B, ssk, knit to end (1 st dec).

Rep last rnd—50 (56, 62, 68) sts. Remove marker B.

Rounded Collar

Change to smaller needles. Knit 12 rnds.

BO loosely. Edge will curl forward, tack down if desired. Weave in all ends.

Buttercup

2					o		o				/	1

Legend

☐ K on RS, P on WS

⊙ YO

◪ K2tog

◩ Ssk

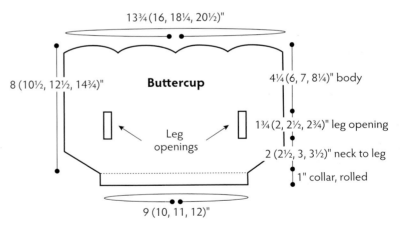

13¾ (16, 18¼, 20½)"

8 (10½, 12½, 14¾)"

4¼ (6, 7, 8¼)" body

Buttercup

Leg openings

1¾ (2, 2½, 2¾)" leg opening

2 (2½, 3, 3½)" neck to leg

1" collar, rolled

9 (10, 11, 12)"

Basic Stitches

Everyone has favorite cast-on, bind-off, and increase methods, including me. I remained faithful to my favorites, using the same techniques for all the patterns in this book. If you have methods that work well for you, go ahead and use them. The look may differ slightly from my sample, but it won't change the integrity of the piece.

Following are the types of stitches I chose, and why.

Cast Ons

I used two different types of cast ons in this book, knitted on and provisional.

Knitted Cast On

The knitted cast on is one of my favorite cast-on methods. It's the easiest to learn, since you are simply making a knit (or purl) stitch. You never have to estimate the length of a yarn tail, because you only use the working yarn.

1. Make a slipknot and place on LH needle. Insert RH needle as if to knit.

2. YO and pull yarn through stitch, as for a regular knit stitch.

3. Place new stitch on LH needle. Repeat process until you've cast on the required number of stitches.

Provisional Cast On

A provisional cast on is worked with a scrap of waste yarn that is later removed. This lets you return to your cast-on edge and work an edging or continue knitting from live stitches, rather than having to pick up stitches. My favorite way to work a provisional cast on is by crocheting a chain over a knitting needle. It's a simple and straightforward way to get evenly spaced cast-on stitches, and you can easily control the stitches when it's time to remove the waste yarn and slip the live stitches onto a needle.

1. Working with waste yarn, make a slipknot and place on crochet hook. Bring yarn to back of LH knitting needle. YO crochet hook and pull through slipknot.

2. Bring waste yarn to back of needle. Pull yarn through loop on hook and bring yarn to back of LH knitting needle. Repeat process until you've cast on necessary number of stitches.

3. Chain five or six stitches, cut waste yarn and pull through last chain loosely. Remove crochet provisional cast on when needed and place live stitches on needle.

Binding Off

I've used the decreasing bind off exclusively for the projects in this book. It's my favorite because it's fast and easy, and I don't have to worry about the bound-off edge being too tight since it's worked at the same gauge as the rest of my knitting.

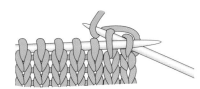

K2tog through back loop and place new stitch from RH needle onto LH needle.

Repeat process until you've bound-off the necessary number of stitches.

Binding Off in Rib

When binding off in a rib pattern, alternate knitting two stitches together through the back loop (K2tog tbl) or purling two stitches together (P2tog) every stitch or every other stitch according to the rib pattern. Move yarn forward to purl or back to knit before the loop is slipped to LH needle.

Increases

I used a lifted increase, also known as the raised increase, in the patterns in this book. This type of increase makes a defined line, thus creating a tailored look. Make one right (M1R) creates a right-slanting increase, while make one left (M1L) leans to the left.

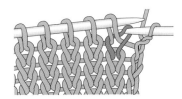

M1R: With RH needle tip, lift the purl bar of stitch directly below first stitch on LH needle. Place lifted stitch onto LH needle and knit or purl new stitch as instructed.

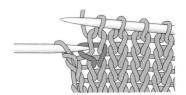

M1L: With LH needle tip, lift the purl bar of stitch directly below stitch just worked on RH needle. Knit or purl new stitch as instructed.

Decreases

The decreases I used in this book are the mirroring right-slanting, knit two stitches together (K2tog), and the left-slanting, slip, slip, knit (ssk).

K2tog: Insert RH needle knitwise into first two sts on LH needle at the same time, working the two stitches as if they were one.

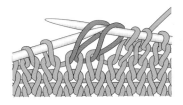

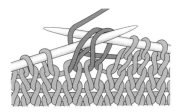

Ssk: Slip first two stitches one at a time from LH needle as if to knit. This will change the direction of the stitches. Knit two remaining stitches together through the back loop.

Abbreviations

[ ]	Work instructions within brackets as many times as directed.
approx	approximately
beg	begin(ning)
BO	bind off
CC	contrasting color
cn	cable needle(s)
CO	cast on
cont	continue(ing)(s)
dec(s)	decrease(ing)(s)
dpn(s)	double-pointed needle(s)
inc(s)	increase(ing)(s)
K	knit
K2tog	knit 2 stitches together—1 stitch decreased
kw	knitwise
LH	left hand
M1	make 1 stitch
MC	main color
oz	ounce(s)
P	purl
P2tog	purl 2 stitches together—1 stitch decreased
patt(s)	pattern(s)
PM	place marker
prev	previous

PU	pick up and knit
pw	purlwise
rem	remain(ing)
rep(s)	repeat(s)
RH	right hand
rnd(s)	round(s)
RS	right side
sl	slip
ssk	slip 2 stitches knitwise, 1 at a time, to right needle, then insert left needle from left to right into front loops and knit 2 stitches together—1 stitch decreased
st(s)	stitch(es)
St st(s)	stockinette stitch(es)
T2R (twist 2 right)	Knit second stitch on left needle, do not remove; knit first stitch on left needle, remove both stitches from left needle
tbl	through the back loop(s)
tog	together
WS	wrong side
wyib	with yarn in back
wyif	with yarn in front
yd(s)	yard(s)
YO(s)	yarn over(s)

Metric Conversion

yards	=	meters	x	1.0936
meters	=	yards	x	0.9144
ounces	=	grams	x	0.0352
grams	=	ounces	x	28.35

Skill Levels

◗□□◖ Beginner:
Projects for first-time knitters using basic knit and purl stitches. Minimal shaping.

◗■□◖ Easy:
Projects using basic stitches, repetitive stitch patterns, and simple color changes. Simple shaping and finishing.

◗■■◖ Intermediate:
Projects using a variety of stitches, such as basic cables and lace, simple intarsia, and techniques for double-pointed needles and knitting in the round. Mid-level shaping and finishing.

◗■■◗ Experienced:
Projects using advanced techniques and stitches, such as short rows, Fair Isle, more intricate intarsia, cables, lace patterns, and numerous color changes.

Standard Yarn-Weight System

Yarn-Weight Symbol and Category Name	0 Lace	1 Super Fine	2 Fine	3 Light	4 Medium	5 Bulky	6 Super Bulky
Types of Yarn in Category	Fingering, 10-count crochet thread	Sock, Fingering, Baby	Sport, Baby	DK, Light Worsted	Worsted, Afghan, Aran	Chunky, Craft, Rug	Bulky, Roving
Knit Gauge Range* in Stockinette Stitch to 4"	33 to 40** sts	27 to 32 sts	23 to 26 sts	21 to 24 sts	16 to 20 sts	12 to 15 sts	6 to 11 sts
Recommended Needle in Metric Size Range	1.5 to 2.25 mm	2.25 to 3.25 mm	3.25 to 3.75 mm	3.75 to 4.5 mm	4.5 to 5.5 mm	5.5 to 8 mm	8 mm and larger
Recommended Needle in US Size Range	000 to 1	1 to 3	3 to 5	5 to 7	7 to 9	9 to 11	11 and larger

*These are guidelines only. The above reflect the most commonly used gauges and needle or hook sizes for specific yarn categories.

**Laceweight yarns are usually knitted or crocheted on larger needles and hooks to create lacy, openwork patterns. Accordingly, a gauge range is difficult to determine. Always follow the gauge stated in your pattern.

Acknowledgments

Thank you to:

My dear husband, Zvi, who got takeout more often than he probably wanted.

My children: Devorah, my cheerleader; Dina, my sounding board; Yosefa, my design consultant; Hillel, my math guru; and Avi, my muse.

Our Hailey (Bear), the reason I needed a dog sweater in the first place.

My size models and their humans: Tara, Mary, and Simeon Carvajal; Snowball, Lianne, and Etiel Forman; ChallieRoll, Nechama, and Yoni Greenfield; Charlie and Queen LaPeefa; Janet and Lior Hod; Ruby, Andria, and Yehuda Rosenbaum.

About the Author

Photograph by Andria Rosenbaum

From a very young age, Sharon Sebrow has enjoyed needlework of all kinds, with guidance from her grandmothers, magazines, and books. As a teacher, Sharon's ultimate joy is seeing the satisfaction of beginners when they successfully use a technique they thought was beyond their capabilities.

In 2004 "Sharon Sews," a question-and-answers column, was published in national quilting magazines. In 2009 Sharon's first book was published, detailing how to make the traditional Kaleidoscope quilt block using her patented template, the Kaleidoscope Smart-Plate®.

Sharon's philosophy is, "If it takes too long, it won't get finished!" She brings her approach of immediate gratification to her projects with seamless knitting and, often, knitting in the round, finishing them in just a few days.